WESTMAR COLLEGE LIBRARY

W9-CES-797

THOMAS EAKINS

The Great American Artists Series

ALBERT P. RYDER *by Lloyd Goodrich*

THOMAS EAKINS *by Fairfield Porter*

WINSLOW HOMER *by Lloyd Goodrich*

WILLEM de KOONING *by Thomas B. Hess*

STUART DAVIS *by E. C. Goossen*

JACKSON POLLOCK *by Frank O'Hara*

IN PREPARATION

JOHN JAMES AUDUBON *by Ruthven Todd*

JOHN MARIN *by Kenneth Sawyer*

BEN SHAHN *by James Thrall Soby*

ARSHILE GORKY *by Harold Rosenberg*

Thomas
EAKINS

by Fairfield Porter

GEORGE BRAZILLER, INC.

NEW YORK   1959

ND
237
.E15
P6

© George Braziller, Inc. 1959

All rights in this book are reserved.
For information address the publisher,
George Braziller, Inc., 215 Fourth Avenue,
New York 3, N.Y.

LIBRARY OF CONGRESS CATALOG CARD NUMBER: 59-12225

PRINTED IN THE UNITED STATES OF AMERICA
BY R. R. DONNELLEY & SONS COMPANY

43979

CONTENTS

THOMAS EAKINS

Anonymous collection

Photograph Philadelphia Museum of Art

EAKINS IS NOT a painter, he is a force,"[1] was the appraisal of Walt Whitman. They first became acquainted when Eakins went to Camden to ask the poet if he would consent to pose for a portrait. The portrait was painted the year after Eakins had been made to resign from his teaching position at the Pennsylvania Academy of Fine Arts because of a disagreement in principle with the governing board. Eakins stuck to his principles and lost his job, and with the loss of his job, he lost a position in the Philadelphia art world.

A great deal is packed into Whitman's appraisal. It implies that a moral quality, a force of character, was more important than Eakins' artistic stature. It implies that a certain moral force is expressed in his paintings, and perhaps that Whitman understood the paradoxical nature of the content of his paintings. Briefly it is this: Eakins used art to express an American sense of life that was essentially anti-artistic. In his life time, he was not a popular painter. His contemporaries were repelled by the severity of his acceptance of the values of his environment. This acceptance was symbolized by the fact that he lived all his life, except for his student days, at the same address.

The society whose values Eakins expressed was a new one engaged in rebuilding the country after the disaster of the American Civil War. From contemporary photographs one notices even in the faces of Northerners a sense of defeat, a recognition of the

9

necessity for self-reliance to replace the youthfulness that the war had destroyed. There was a break with tradition: the war had separated us from our past. Although the condition of the country after the war was already implicit in the many rapid changes that had gone on before it, changes based on the Westward expansion, on the struggle for dominance between North and South, and the beginning of the Industrial Revolution, still, before the war the artistic expression of the country dated back to Colonial times, behind which stood the Italian Renaissance. In the visual arts and in industrial design there was a petering out of this energy and a perfection of taste. James Jackson Jarves (1818–1888) wrote: "The American, while adhering closely to his utilitarian and economical principles, has unwittingly, in some objects to which his heart equally with his hand has been devoted, developed a degree of beauty in them that no other nation equals. His clipper ships, fire-engines, locomotives, and some of his machinery and tools combine that equilibrium of line, proportions and masses which are among the causes of abstract beauty. Their success in producing broad general effects out of a few simple elements, and of admirable adaptations of means to ends, as nature evolves beauty out of the common and practical, covers these things with a certain atmosphere of poetry, and is an indication of what may happen to the rest of his work when he puts into it an equal amount of heart and knowledge."[2] And some of this taste survived the war. For instance, after the war, Santayana as a boy came to live in Boston with his American mother. He recalled, as if it were a symbol of his new environment, the slender functional elegance of the wagon that met them at the wharf.

As Eakins was the typical painter of the decades after the war, so Samuel F. B. Morse (1791–1872) was the painter for the society that preceded it. His life expressed the pre-Civil War artistic dependence of this country on European tradition, and also the beginning of the change in American life that the war consummated. Morse's painting was on a very high level: he had taste and a control of the medium comparable to his European contemporaries.

10

His portrait of President Monroe is more ambitious than Gilbert Stuart's and superior to it. But *The House of Representatives,* a large and masterly work which he painted later, shows less energy. The good taste of tradition and the skill of innocence which it displays might be compared to the freshness and balance of Madison's political thinking when he was a delegate to the Constitutional Convention. The House of Representatives embodies the egalitarian ideas of the Convention, and it does not quite work to paint it in a style established by and expressive of a hierarchical society. The picture lacks conviction. "The confusion between good taste and anemia that has so often characterized American life"[3] may have had its beginnings in such works as this one. In any case Morse gave up painting, and he is best remembered for the invention of the telegraph. His career illustrates a failure of artistic nerve, the consequence of being born at the wrong time and in the wrong place.

With Morse, science supplanted art based on tradition. On the other hand, Eakins deliberately based his art on science. It is not a relation to tradition that validates Eakins' paintings, but their origin in natural logic. Eakins' nerve was adequate to a greater challenge than Morse's: he had neither Morse's skill nor his interest in the art of the past, and though his work did not suffer from the particular anemia of good taste, it began out of something like spiritual exhaustion—a rigidity that followed from fulfilling the demands of an inorganic conscience. And it took him most of his life to overcome this. The science of the two painters differs in the same way that their paintings do—Morse's science has the wonder and delight of the Humanists, while Eakins' is full of technique and discipline. Morse found the study of electricity artistic, but Eakins reversed this, and for him science was practical.

All his life Eakins liked to read mathematics, and advised his pupils to study higher mathematics, because it was "so like painting."[4] He kept a blackboard in his dining room to aid discussion, and a well-equipped metal and wood-working shop on the top floor. When he was a schoolboy he constructed a steam engine that ran. In high school, he liked to make mechanical drawings of com-

11

plicated machinery, and perspective drawings of geometrical solids. An exercise that he set his advanced students was to represent a boat under sail. He had them use mechanical drawing instruments, first rendering the circumscribed brick shape that had three inclinations: to the picture-plane, to the direction of the wind, to the waves. He said a boat was like the human figure. This exercise combined almost all the problems that a student would have to meet and that Eakins lectured about: anatomy, perspective and reflections. Like many practical people who think of knowledge as a means, it was the means that he enjoyed. He liked tools and he liked facts for their own sake. He had a great gift for language; he knew French perfectly and he identified himself with it so completely that his letters home from Paris during his student days were full of French locutions, such as "gave us to drink" and "gentlemen repressing the curiosity of the little children."[5] But he identified himself with the structure of the language, not French culture. Once, visiting a convent with his friend and pupil Samuel Murray, the others were astonished that he carried on a conversation with some Chinese monks. He was talking to them in Latin. Though he liked mathematics, he refused to take stock in "poetical" mathematics, saying to someone who tried to interest him in the fourth dimension, "You can't tie a knot in the fourth dimension"[6] (which is true, since a knot in the fourth dimension is no more secure than a loop in the third).

His preoccupation with the useful did not include an appreciation for art. He cared nothing for fiction, and was more like a sensitive business man who is skeptical and even contemptuous of the "artistic," but may be deeply moved by one outstanding work. Eakins' reading outside of mathematics was limited to Dante, Rabelais and Whitman, whom he read over and over again. If he was to waste his time, as he later admitted doing in his too thorough study of anatomy, he preferred to do it paying attention to actualities.

After he graduated from high school at the age of sixteen with an A.B. degree, he studied drawing at the Pennsylvania Academy

12

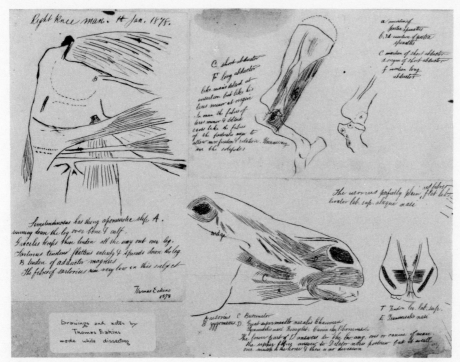

Photograph Philadelphia Museum of Art

of Fine Arts and anatomy at Jefferson Medical School. Anatomy, the factual side of medicine, fascinated him so much that he considered becoming a surgeon. He continued to dissect cadavers in Paris at the Beaux Arts. After returning to America, he dissected at Jefferson College again, and continued doing so as a professor of anatomy at the Pennsylvania Academy. He urged his pupils to dissect from the cadaver, though he shared their natural dislike for it. "I don't know of anyone who doesn't dislike it," he said. "Every fall, for my part, I feel a great reluctance to begin it . . . we had a student who abstained a year ago, but finding his fellows were getting along faster than himself, he changed his mind . . . " "One dissects simply to increase his knowledge of how beautiful objects are put together to the end that he may be able to imitate them. Ever to refine upon natural beauty—to idealize—one must under-

13

stand what he is idealizing, otherwise his idealization—I don't like the word, by the way—becomes distortion, and distortion is ugliness. This whole matter of dissection is not art at all any more than grammar is poetry. It is work, and hard work, disagreeable work . . . Of course one can waste time over anatomy and dissection. I did when I began to study . . . for a time my attention to anatomy hampered me."[7]

Eakins' interest in anatomy and physiology led him to original research. He read a paper before the Philadelphia Academy of Sciences *On the Differential Action of Certain Muscles Passing more than One Joint*. He stated: "I was surprised to observe in the strain of starting a horse car that the so-called flexors and extensors were in strong action at the same time." This discovery disproved the contention of physiologists that each muscle has a single function countered by its opposite muscle (i. e., each flexor countered by an extensor) and that muscular action consists of a sequence of separate actions. To test his observation, he made a model out of rubber bands and levers; and he found that when he had dissected away all the muscles from a dead horse's legs, the tendons alone were able to hold the leg so rigid as to support weight. "The hoof pieces properly set upon the ground, the leg stood firm, all tendency to collapse being prevented by the leverage of tendons passing the joints . . . I denuded a front and back leg of all muscle fibre, and the legs sustained weight. An increase in weight increased the resistance." He concluded that "the least action anywhere is carried through the whole animal. The differential action of the muscles secures to the scapula from which the horse's body hangs, a much longer and swifter throw, a concurrent and auxiliary movement of great muscles, generally supposed to be antagonistic, a grace and harmony that any less perfect system of co-ordination would surely miss."[8]

Another of Eakins' scientific projects was a series of experiments in photographing moving animals and athletes—carried out in 1884 under the auspices of the University of Pennsylvania—that was to prove important in the development of the motion-picture

14

camera. He was stimulated by the work of Eadweard Muybridge, commissioned by Governor Stanford of California to settle a bet with sporting friends about the nature of a horse's gait. Eakins suggested, first, that instead of lines on the ground behind the horse, Muybridge should photograph a grid over the track after the animal had run, to avoid complicated calculations in perspective; and second, that Muybridge should photograph the separate positions from one fixed camera, instead of from 24 cameras in a row, as he had done. A French physiologist, E. J. Marey, had already tried to accomplish this by using a disk shutter pierced by several openings revolving before the lens. Eakins used two smaller disks, one revolving eight times as fast as the other, which reduced the dimensions of the apparatus. He designed and built this revolving apparatus himself and also calculated the correct refractions for the lenses.

Eakins' scruples made him dislike the word "idealize," which in so far as it meant changing nature, could mean distortion, namely, ugliness. By investigating the true function of muscles, he found true beauty. His criticisms of Muybridge came from a sensitive appreciation of the limitations of the camera as an instrument for discovering fact. He made a gray copy of *The Fairman Rogers Four-in-Hand* to be photographed, in place of the original in full color, since before the invention of the panchromatic film photography translated color values inaccurately.

His personal attachments had the constancy of his unchanging environment. As the eldest child and only son he easily identified himself with his father, and developed a very domineering character.[9] His father, Benjamin Eakins, was a writing master, and penmanship was the first step in Eakins' artistic apprenticeship. His father lived with him all his life. They spent a lot of time together engaged in all kinds of individualistic outdoor sports—swimming, sailing, hunting and skating. Benjamin Eakins was an excellent skater, tracing calligraphic flourishes on the ice. Thomas could skate backwards as fast as most people could forwards. His father was a man of independent mind, a free-thinker and a Democrat

15

during the Civil War, without much enthusiasm for the Northern cause.

When Eakins lost his job at the Academy, almost all his pupils remained loyal to him and organized the Philadelphia Art Students' League so that they might continue to study with him. Samuel Murray became his pupil at the Art Students' League; and at this point in his career, when he needed allies, a friendship started that was in the last half of Eakins' life a mirror image of the relationship with his father in the first half. Murry shared Eakin's studio for ten years, and he introduced Eakins to the world of boxing, of wrestling, and the Catholic Church.

When Eakins went to Paris, one of the first of the advance-guard of Americans to study in France instead of in London, the teacher who attracted him was Gèrôme, the dominating spirit of the Beaux Arts. After only a month he was admitted to Gérôme's classes, a great honor for a foreigner. Gérôme's clear teaching methods emphasized the careful rendering of the literal truth. In Gérôme's paintings the sense of proportion is a sense of the equality of parts, the drawing is everywhere equally sharp and the color is local color. It is a vulgarization of Ingres, and it denies subjectivity. Gérôme's paintings have the pettiness and perfection of mechanical drawings which enable a model-maker to produce a doll-sized version of a scene. As an art student Eakins was only interested in the academicians. He rarely visited the Louvre or the Luxembourg, and at the Paris Exposition of 1867 he commented only on the beauty of the American locomotive. In Madrid, all he noticed about Titian's paintings was that there were no cracks in the shadows. Though he had to learn from experience how to handle the oil medium, he admired the ability of the academicians in solving practical problems of representation. With their modest aims and their lack of feeling for tradition, they took their calling to be equivalent to a kind of manufacture, and this fitted very well to Eakins' post-Civil War provincialism. It was as though there were no valid precedents to lean on. And indeed this was almost the case. Paris differed from

16

Philadelphia for him chiefly in that in Paris there were many more art students.

Eakins' sense of his own identity was balanced by high moral standards and a strict conscience. He wrote to his father accounting for every penny that his father sent him. At his father's protest against such scrupulousness, Eakins wrote, "Spending your money, which came to you from hard work, I am touched by the delicacy of your not wanting the items but only the sum left, but I will continue to give them as I have always done."[10]

He purchased a copy of Rabelais, "a writer, priest, doctor of medicine and hater of the priesthood. He wrote a very fine book which I bought and am now reading."[11]

When tradition failed as the justification for art, conscientiousness became its shaky substitute. For it is a confession of doubt about the validity of art. The modesty of the French academicians fitted Eakins' American doubt of art, of religion, of any meaning to life than went further than its efficient maintenance. His studies were to be used towards "picture-making," which he later told his pupils "should not be put off too long." "There are men in Paris in the schools who paint day after day from the model. They never try to paint anything else . . . They are now old men. They cannot paint as well as they could twenty years ago."[12] His distrust of spontaneity, which is the reverse of conscientiousness, shows in his estimate of the value of "studies": "The French boys sometimes learn to make wonderful fine studies, but I notice [they] seldom make good pictures, for to make these wonderful studies they must . . . pay all their attention to what they are putting on their canvas rather than in their heads." "The study maker . . . must paint at the first lick . . . so that a wonderful study is an accomplishment and not power . . . The best artists never make . . . flashy studies."[13]

As tradition seemed inadequate as a basis for art, so did traditional rhetoric, which to Eakins was simply dishonest. He wrote to his father from Madrid about Rubens: "I always hated his nasty vulgar work and now I have seen the best he ever did, I can hate

17

him too. The best picture he ever painted stands by a Velasquez. His best quality, that of light on flesh, is knocked by Velasquez, and that is Rubens' only quality, while it is but the beginning of Velasquez' . . . [Rubens'] men are twisted to pieces. His modelling is always crooked and dropsical and no marking is ever in the right place or anything like what he sees in nature, his people never have bones, his color is dashing and flashy, his people must all be in the most violent action, must use the strength of Hercules if a little watch is to be wound up, the wind must be blowing great guns in a chamber or dining room, everything must be making a noise and tumbling about, there must be monsters too, for his men are not monstrous enough for him. His pictures put me in mind of chamber pots and I would not be sorry if they were all burnt."[14]

Such vehemence comes from an offended conscience. It is like Mark Twain's objection to Raphael's putting three men in a boat that wouldn't hold a dog. Mark Twain had the same sort of conscience as Eakins—a conscience that was greatly shocked by whatever denied the supremacy of fact—but because he turned his offense into a joke (what is not true is funny), he became, as Eakins did not, a very popular and successful artist.

Eakins was stubborn. For example, from Zermat, below the Matterhorn, in beautiful mountain scenery, he wrote that the country was "the most God-forsaken place I ever saw or hope to see. The people are all either cretins or only half cretins with the goiter on their necks. They live in the filthiest manner possible, the lower apartment being privy and barn combined and they breed by incest altogether . . . If I was a military conqueror and they were in my way I would burn every hovel and spare nobody for fear they would contaminate the rest of the world."[15] A friend once came upon Eakins studying a Whistler painting of a little girl, and asked him what he thought of it. Eakins turned around, "I think it is a very cowardly way to paint." The friend asked if he did not find that it had a charm and beauty, and Eakins turned back to the painting, saying that he had not thought of that.[16]

He went to Spain in 1869 and there he painted his first com-

18

posed picture, as distinct from studies, *Street Scene in Seville* (plate 4). "Picture making is new to me; there is the sun and gay colors and a hundred things you never see in studio light, and ever so many botherations that no one out of the trade could ever guess at . . . What I have arrived at I have not gained without hard plodding work. My studies and worries have made me thin. For a long time I did not hardly sleep at nights, but dreamed all the time about colors and forms, and often nearly always they were crazinesses in their queerness [sic] . . . How I suffered in my doubting and would change again, make a fine drawing and rub weak sickly color on it, and if my comrades or my teacher told me it was better, it most drove me crazy, and again I would go back to my old instinct and make frightful work again. It made me doubt of myself, of my intelligence, of everything, and yet I thought things looked so beautiful and clear that I need not be mistaken. I think I tried every road possible. Sometimes I took all advice, sometimes I shut my ears and listened to none. My worst troubles are over, I know perfectly what I am doing and can run my modelling, without polishing or sneaking it away to the end. I can finish as far as I can see. What a relief to me when I saw everything falling in its place, as I always had an instinct that it would if I could ever get my bearings all correct at once."[17] The difficulty of painting was more important to him than his pleasure in sunlight and color.

From Madrid he wrote of his enthusiasm for Spanish painting. "I have seen big paintings here . . . the good Spanish work . . . so strong, so reasonable, so free from every affectation."[18] Velasquez and Ribera were free of the rhetoric he despised in Rubens. He admired Rembrandt also, but not the Dutch school in general. "The big artist does not sit down monkey-like and copy a coal scuttle or an ugly old woman like some Dutch painters have done . . . but he keeps a sharp eye on Nature and steals her tools. He learns what she does with light, the big tool, and then color, then form. . . . The big artists . . . had the greatest confidence in nature, and when they made an unnatural thing they made it as nature would have made it, and thus they are really closer to nature than the coal-

19

scuttle painters ever suspect. In a big picture you can see what o'clock it is, whether morning or afternoon, if it is hot or cold, winter or summer and what kind of people are there and what they are doing and why . . . The sentiments run beyond words. If a man makes a hot day he makes it like a hot day he once saw or is seeing; if a sweet face, a face he once saw or which he imagines from old memories and his knowledge, and he combines, never creates—but at the very first combination no man, and least of all himself could ever disentangle the feelings that animated him just then, and refer each one to its right place." [19] It is as though he thought creation synonymous to affectation and as suspect as accomplishment.

The French academicians painted "machines," that is, deliberate, elaborate paintings of great size whose purpose was the display of the artist's powers. Eakins thought of painting as a deliberate construction. His paintings of scullers were executed from studies of perspective, of reflections and of anatomy put together in the studio. An Eakins "machine" was more modest and thorough than a French academician's; it was a fixation of an idea on canvas, like the *Concert Singer* (plate 44). He posed the model in exactly the same position every day relative to a grid placed vertically behind her, with a place on the wall in front for her to look at. He attached colored ribbons to salient points of the dress corresponding to points on the grid. The canvas was perpendicular to the floor and at right angles to the eye of the painter. The painting became a projection of the figure on a vertical plane, like an architect's elevation. He went through these anguished accuracies because he trusted his head more than his hand and knowledge more than appearance.

What he thought, was derived from what he did, and he taught his pupils his own practice. The profound seriousness of his teaching impressed the public, and his school became known. His pupils revered him. He hardly ever praised, but was never sharp or sarcastic. If he liked a student's work, his face lit up, "You are now there; with an effort you will do good work." [20] Robert Henri, himself an inspiring teacher, said: "It was an excitement to hear his pupils talk of him. They believed in him as a great master, and there

20

Anonymous collection

THOMAS EAKINS

were stories of his power, his will in the pursuit of study, his unwavering adherence to his ideals, his great willingness to give, to help, and the pleasure he had in seeing the original and the worthy crop out in a student's work" [21]

Fairman Rogers, Eakins' friend and admirer and a director of the Pennsylvania Academy of Fine Arts, wrote an account of the school: "Mr. Eakins teaches that the great masses of the body are the first thing that should be put upon the canvas in preference to the outline . . . the students build up their figures from the inside rather than fill them up after having lined in the outside . . . it is not believed that the difficulties of painting are either lessened or more quickly surmounted by the substitution of arbitrary colors, black and white, for the true colors; . . . the comparison with nature is more direct and close [than would be the case if pencil or charcoal were used instead of paint] . . .

"The accurate knowledge of anatomy obtained through lectures and dissections forms a strong basis for the intelligent rendering of . . . character . . . Conventionalizing, or imposing on the model, is discouraged, as the object is study and not picture-making; and the use of a variety of models familiarizes the student with many different types . . . One peculiarity of the school, which has been unfavorably criticised, is that there is little variety in the instruction; that is the student's work is through casts, which are almost universally of the nude human figure; they then enter the life class and continue to work from the nude human figure, usually in simple poses, and then they work in the dissecting room, also from the human figure . . . There is the objection that the school does not sufficiently teach the students picture-making, and it may be met by saying that it is hardly within the province of the school to do so. It is better learned outside . . .

"The anatomical study is so much more complete than in other schools, that it requires special notice . . . the cadaver is used in preference to manikins, since it is the original material." [22]

In the women's class Eakins removed the loin cloth from a male model to demonstrate the origin of a muscle. His scientific earnestness conflicted with propriety: he refused to compromise, and he was fired. "Respectability in art is appalling,"[23] he had said on another occasion. All but 12 of his pupils signed a petition for his return. The Governing Board, no longer counting Fairman Rogers among them, felt that in the face of an annual deficit, it was presumptuous of the students to tell them what to do. *The Philadelphia Evening Bulletin* (Feb. 16, 1886) came out for propriety: "Mr. Eakins has for a long time entertained and strongly inculcated the most 'advanced' views . . . teaching large classes of women as

22

well as men, he holds that, both as to the living model in the drawing room and the dead subject in the anatomical lecture and dissecting room, Art knows no sex. He has pressed this always disputed doctrine with much zeal and with much success, until he has impressed it so strongly upon a majority of the young men that they have sided with him when he has pushed his views to their last logical illustration by compelling or seeking to compel the women entrusted to his direction to face the absolute nude. That the women of the life school should have revolted at the tests forced upon them was inevitable."[24]

Though he kept the esteem of his pupils and an intelligent minority, his career was set back by his following his views to their "last logical illustration." When a Philadelphia hostess asked Sargent whom he would like her to ask to dinner, and Sargent replied, "There's Eakins, for instance," she asked, "Who's Eakins?" His sitters often disliked the way he painted them, though Whitman was a notable exception (plate 49). A. W. Lee (plate 72) paid for but refused to accept the portrait he had commissioned. Many of his portraits were of friends, and made "for the love of art" as one of the priests whom he painted wrote in a letter (*The Translator,* not reproduced). Neither Dr. Gross nor Dr. Agnew liked his showing blood on their hands. *The Gross Clinic* (plate 21) earned him the reputation of "butcher." A Philadelphia critic wrote of this painting that "the more one praises it the more one must condemn its admission to a gallery where men and women of weak nerves must be compelled to look at it, for not to look at it is impossible."[25]

All the criticisms of his work that had been made during his life time were restated by British critics on the occasion of an American exhibition in London in 1946. B. L. D. Thomas wrote, "a painter who looks like living up to the requirements of a man of independence is Thomas Eakins . . . with his downright realism . . . [which] is unfortunately rather a negation of art . . . Although he studied for four years in Europe, his painting remained labored and provincial so that he fails to achieve greatness either by felicities of observation and handling like Courbet, or by an underlying mood

23

of deep poetry like Caravaggio." Cyril Connolly was wittier: "It is no good pretending that . . . Eakins . . . can hold a cuspidor to [Whistler, Cassatt and Sargent]. There is no doubt that for the great ones the climate of this new dollar-glutted America was unbearable."[26] (The "great ones" were the expatriates.)

There have always been other opinions; for instance when The *Gross Clinic* was first exhibited, an anonymous critic wrote: "The public of Philadelphia now have, for the first time, an opportunity to form something like an accurate judgement with regard to the qualities of an artist who in many particulars is very far in advance of his American rivals . . . we know of nothing in the history of portraiture that has been attempted in this city, or indeed in this country, that in any way approaches it." And it is true that Eakins was the outstanding primitive of the American society that began to develop in 1865. Whitman gave his opinion of the qualities of Eakins, both as a painter and as a man, in conversations with friends.

In 1887, shortly after being fired from his teaching job at the Academy, Eakins went to see Whitman to ask to paint his portrait. Whitman agreed, and an acquaintance began between them. Whitman got to like the portrait more and more. At first he had been afraid that it looked glum: "That is its one doubtful feature; if I though it would finally look glum I would hate it." Instead, he found that "it is not seen all at once—it only dawns on you gradually . . . the more I get to realize it the profounder seems its insight.

"I never knew but one artist, and that's Tom Eakins, who could resist the temptation to see what they think ought to be rather than what is.

"The Eakins portrait . . . sets me down in correct style without feathers . . . it never . . . weakens.

"Tom's portraits, which the formalists, the academic people won't have at any price . . . are not a remaking of life but life, its manifests, just as it is, as they are."[27]

And, speaking of Eakins as a man, in answer to a question whether Eakins were uncouth, uncharitable, boorish, lacking the

24

Private collection

Arcadia. 1883. Bronze relieve, 12½ x 25″.

social graces, what Whitman expressed was in essence Eakins' whole feeling about life and art: it explains the nature of his paintings and their appearance. "Eakins does wear well, he is a good comrade. What are social gifts? The parlor puts quite its own measure upon social gifts. I should say, Tom Eakins lacks them as, for instance, it would be said that I lack them: not that they are forgotten, despised, but that they enter secondarily upon the affairs of my life. Eakins might put it this way: first there is this thing to do, then this other thing, then maybe a third thing or this fourth: these done, got out of the way, *now* the social graces . . . he does not dismiss them but puts them in their place."[28] First came facts and science; the social graces symbolized art, tradition and, last of all, rhetoric. "Eakins has no parlor gallantries, but something vastly better. At first sight he might be taken to be negative in quality, manner, intuition, but that surface impression wears off after a few

25

meetings."[29] It seems that Eakins was one of the first American artists to adopt, as it were in apology, something very close to what James Truslow Adams called "the mucker pose."

He was the first American artist—as distinct from craftsman or folk-artist—to make his paintings out of what was there instead of relying greatly on tradition. He was the first of consequence to study in France instead of England. The teacher he chose, though an honored member of French society, was outside of the main tradition. The qualities that earned him adoration and respect were high-mindedness, conscientiousness and an uncompromising willingness to face uncertainty about whether life had meaning. His difficulty was that morality is not art. The rhetoric he despised was inapplicable to the world he both accepted and chose. His wife was an admiring pupil, first attracted to him when she saw *The Gross Clinic;* she was a woman from an even freer-thinking background than his own. He understood Whitman's rhetoric—"Whitman never makes a mistake," he said—a rhetoric that comes out of American newspaper editorials. Truth precluded the formality of "picture-making" as well as the spontaniety of accomplishment, which is to say that the analysis of science precludes the synthesis or spontaneity of art. It precludes "creation" and paying attention to what goes on on the canvas. His conscientiousness towards facts (he had to find as many planes as possible, he had to finish) did not make him trust his senses: "you can copy a thing to a certain limit. Then you must use intellect."[30] The intellect was no organizer, but a protector of the purity of fact against the wind of affectation.

He was commissioned to paint the portrait of President Hayes, and the portrait, which is lost, disappointed his clients. He showed a man at work at his desk, instead of a symbol of the leader of his country, as Morse had done of Monroe.

His clients did not want art to express their lives, any more than they wanted religion to do so: art and religion were for the uninhabited spare room and spare day, for the parlor, for Sunday.

Eakins' career was a *tour-de-force:* he tried to make an art for a society that did not believe in anything beyond material facts.

26

He tried to make something that would give this materialism meaning. Composition is his weakest point; there is almost no formality to his paintings, but an investigation of form that refuses to leave anythng out (as Whistler left things out), and that prefers no one aspect of nature to another.

His acceptance of America's disinterest in art shocked those people who unconsciously agreed with him. He wanted to make art for a new society that had not yet got to the point of having any. What he learned through science, he learned as though no artist had had such problems before him. He tried to make art acceptable to himself by the thoroughness of his learning and his practical skills. And so he puts the burden of disproof on the spectator, whom he challenges to find that this art, expressing the spectator's disbelief in art, is not valid. If he can make an art for those who care nothing for it, if he can express this, what objections can they possibly have? Like the clients of his portraits, America of the Brown Decades was shown itself, and like many of his clients, it did not like the version it saw. His portrait of America does not flatter. But did Eakins find it unflattering, or did he find it beautiful because it was in accordance with nature? He is supposed to have said, "How beautiful an old lady's skin is. All those wrinkles!"

Eakins made an effort to conform his taste to what actually was. In so far as he succeeded, he isolated himself. His crucified Christ (plate 29) was beauty destroyed in isolation. His inner life was like an Indian wrestle in which the force of his domineering character was opposed by the power of a destructive conscience. Often the struggle between these forces led to immobility. Gérôme remarked about a watercolor of a sculler Eakins sent him from Philadelphia, that since he had chosen the central point of the stroke, the result was immobility. It led to darkness. The light in his paintings is hardly pervasive; even in *Max Schmidt in a Single Scull* (plate 8) the dark accents win out. It led to a conscientiousness about detail on one side and an insistence that everything with its load of detail be properly related to the ground, that figures have bones, that weight be supported. It led to his insistence on

27

the primacy of thinking and was expressed in a talent for mathematics (which "you can't fool"). It required him to consider that beauty must be paid for in order to be justified. It is paid for by courage and by difficulties; it is justified by scrupulousness in conformity to nature; things must be finished.

Once he executed some relief panels for a client, who asked that they be left unfinished. Eakins wrote a long explanation as to why this would not do. In the eyes of most of his sitters there is a defeated look that goes beyond objective realism. This is not only the weariness of holding still, it is partly the tribute paid to his conscience for the enjoyment of painting. Because his father's money enabled him not to have to work for a living, he had to convince his conscience that painting was work.

What he could have done with a more selfish character and a weaker conscience is manifest in the sketches; in Sketch for *The Gross Clinic* (plate 20), in some of his unfinished paintings, in the portraits of *Charles Linford* (plate 50), of *Mrs. Gilbert Parker* (plate 80), of *Walt Whitman* (plate 49). Or it shows in a pleasure in light in *Maybelle* (plate 53), or in the relaxed, confident brushing of *Salutat* (plate 57). He composed several figures best when he could identify himself with the painting, as in *The Artist and His Father Hunting Reeds Birds* (not reproduced). His conscience wins in the portrait of his wife, *The Lady with the Setter Dog* (plate 36), a repainting after ten years of the first version, which was a much larger spirited and less severe painting altogether.[31]

If he had been able to apply his intellect in a more unhampered way to the problems of art, he would have produced works of a grace and painterliness surpassing Whistler. The second and third versions of William Rush and his model (plates 76, 77) are more relaxed than the first one (plate 25). His last paintings are freest, without any sacrifice of his sure drawing. But America did not want, in the nineteenth century, what Pre-Raphaelite London or Impressionist Paris might better have appreciated, and Eakins himself eschewed the grace of accomplishment in favor of the rigidity of power. Eakins did not want to transcend his environment, in fact

28

Anonymous collection

LAST PHOTOGRAPH OF THOMAS EAKINS

43979

he could not even imagine transcending it. If it rejected him, his difficulty was that he could not reject it, but had to try to prove, if only to his friends and himself, that he really fitted in harmoniously. He was rejected in his life time because society could not forgive him for accepting it as it was, instead of offering it a picture of something better. Eakins was outside of his time because his intuition was hindsight: what society had missed seeing, was what Eakins saw when it was already beginning to be too late—as a dying man is said to see his whole life clearly pass in review.

NOTES TO THE TEXT

1. Horace Traubel, *With Walt Whitman in Camden* (Boston, 1906–1953) 4 vols.
2. Lewis Mumford, *The Brown Decades* (New York, Dover Publications, Inc.)
3. *ibid.*
4. Lloyd Goodrich, *Thomas Eakins, His Life and Work* (New York, Whitney Museum, 1933)
5. *ibid.*
6. *ibid.*
7. *ibid.*
8. *Proceedings of the Academy of Natural Science of Philadelphia,* (1894)
9. Margaret McHenry, *Thomas Eakins, Who Painted* (privately issued, Oreland, Pa., 1946)
10. Goodrich, *op. cit.*
11. *ibid.*
12. Charles Bregler, "Thomas Eakins as a Teacher," *The Arts,* March and Oct. 1931
13. Goodrich, *op. cit.*
14. McHenry, *op. cit.*
15. *ibid.*
16. *ibid.*
17. Goodrich, *op. cit.*
18. *ibid.*
19. *ibid.*
20. McHenry, *op. cit.*
21. Goodrich, *op. cit.*
22. McHenry, *op. cit.*
23. Goodrich, *op. cit.*
24. *ibid.*
25. *ibid.*
26. *The Burlington Magazine,* Sept. 1946

27. Traubel, *op. cit.*
28. *ibid.*
29. *ibid.*
30. Goodrich, *op. cit.*
31. The first version is reproduced in M. G. Van Rensselaer, *Book of American Figure Painters* (Philadelphia, 1886)

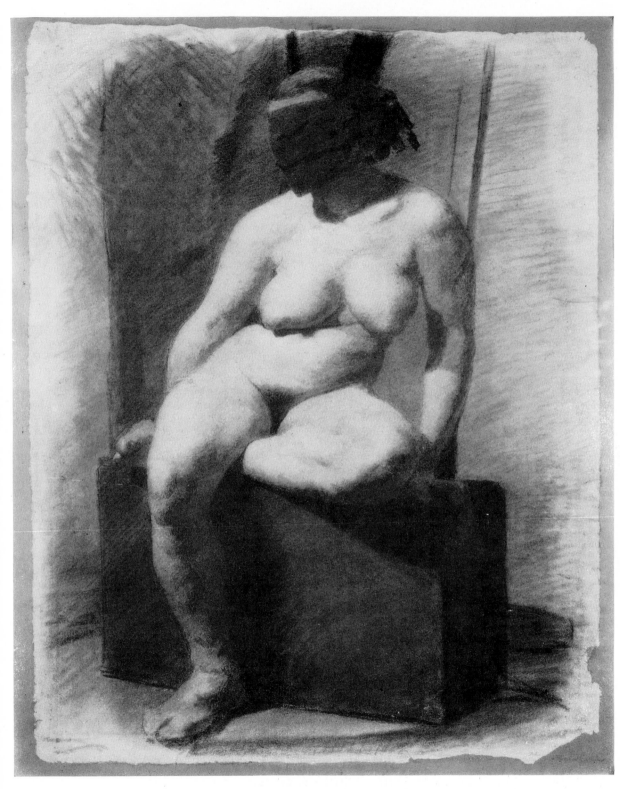

1. *Masked Nude*. 1866. Drawing, 24 x 18″. Philadelphia Museum of Art

2. *Head of Young Woman.* 1867. 18½ x 15¼". Collection unknown

3. *Study of a Girl's Head.* 1867-69. 21½ x 18″. Philadelphia Museum of Art

4. *Street Scene in Seville.* 1870. 5'3" x 3'½". Collection Mrs. Rebecca M. Garrett

5. *Home Scene*. 1871. 21¾ x 18". In the Brooklyn Museum Collection

6. *Margaret.* 1871. 24 x 20". Collection Mr. John H. Mitchell

7. *Marguerite in Skating Costume.* 1871. 24 x 20½″. Philadelphia Museum of Art

8. *Max Schmitt in a Single Scull*. 1871. 32¼ x 46½″. The Metropolitan Museum of Art, Alfred N. Punnett Fund and Gift of George D. Pratt, 1934

9. *Katherine.* 1872. 5'2½" x 4'2". Collection Mr. Stephen C. Clark

10. *The Oarsmen*. 1872. 24 x 36". Philadelphia Museum of Art

11. *Turning Stake Boat.* 1873. 40¼ x 60¼″. The Cleveland Museum of Art, Hinman B. Hurlbut Collection

12. *Oarsmen on the Skuylkill.* 1873. 27 x 47½". In the Brooklyn Museum Collection, J. B. Woodward Memorial Fund

16. *On the Delaware.* 1874. 10 x 17". Collection Mr. Henry Schnakenberg

15. *Sailboats Racing on the Delaware*. 1874. 24⅛ x 36⅛″. Philadelphia Museum of Art

14. *Benjamin Howard Rand*. 1874. 5 x 4′. Jefferson Medical College

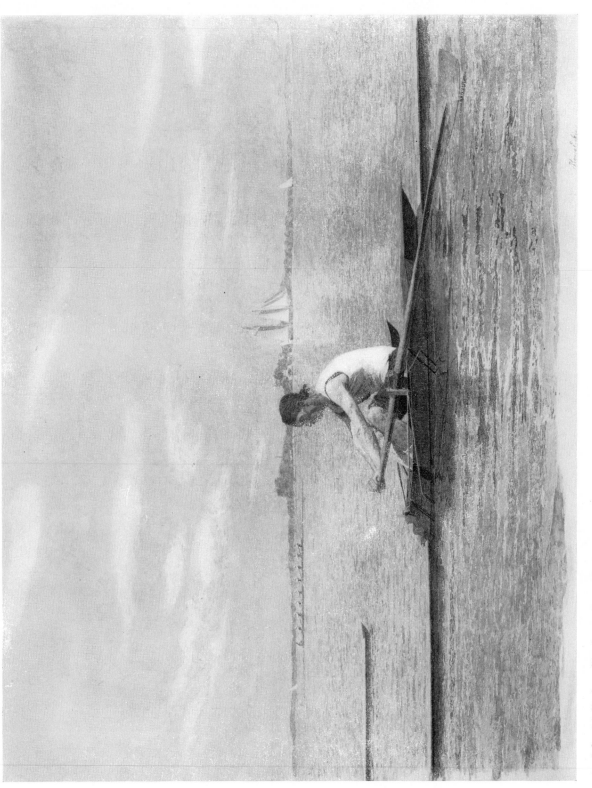

13. *John Biglin in a Single Scull.* 1873. Watercolor, 16¾ x 23″. The Metropolitan Museum of Art

17. *Starting Out After Rail.* 1874. Watercolor, 25 x 20″. Roland P. Murdoch Collection, Wichita Art Museum

18. *Elizabeth at the Piano*. 1875. 6′ x 4′. Addison Gallery of American Art, Phillips Academy, Andover

19. *Baseball Players*. 1875. Watercolor, 9⅜ x 10½″. Rhode Island School of Design

20. Sketch for *The Gross Clinic*. 1875. 24 x 20″. Philadelphia Museum of Art

21. *The Gross Clinic.* 1875. 8′ x 6′6″. Jefferson Medical College

22. *Chess Players*. 1876. 11¾″ x 16¾″. The Metropolitan Museum of Art, Gift of the Artist, 1881

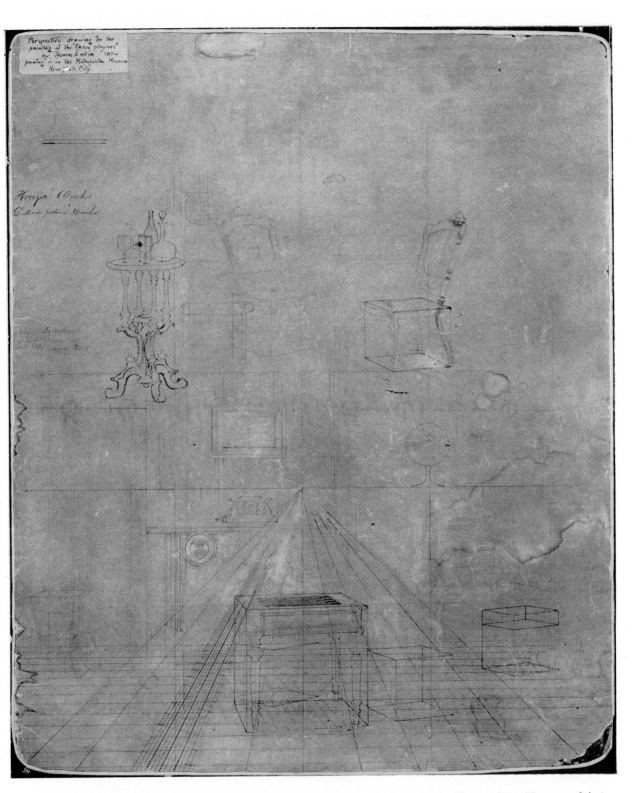

23. Perspective drawing for *Chess Players*. 1876. Pencil and ink on cardboard. The Metropolitan Museum of Art, Fletcher Fund, 1942

24. *Baby at Play.* 1876. 32¼ x 48". Collection Ambassador and Mrs. John Hay Whitney

25. *William Rush Carving the Allegorical Figure of the Skuylkill River*. 1877. 20⅛ x 26½″. Philadelphia Museum of Art

26. *Will Schuster and Black Man Going Shooting.* 1876. 22 x 30″. Collection Mr. Stephen C. Clark

27. *Dr. John H. Brinton.* 1878. 12¼ x 20⅛″. Medical Museum of the Armed Forces, Institute of Pathology

28. *Fairman Rogers Four-in-Hand*. 1879. 24 x 36". Philadelphia Museum of Art

29. *Crucifixion*. 1880. 8′ x 4′6″. Philadelphia Museum of Art

30. *Nude Back.* 1882. 24 x 20". Babcock Galleries

31. *Professionals at Rehearsal.* 1883. 16 x 12″. Philadelphia Museum of Art

32. *Swimming Hole.* 1883. 27 x 36″. Fort Worth Art Center

33. *Youth playing Fife*. 1883. 10 x 8". Collection Mr. Maurice Horwitz

34. *An Arcadian*. 1883. 14 x 18". Collection Mr. Lloyd Goodrich

35. *Mrs. William Shaw Word*. 1884. 40 x 30". Collection Mr. T. Edward Hanley

36. *A Lady with a Setter dog (Mrs. Eakins)*. 1885. 30 x 23". The Metropolitan Museum of Art, Fletcher Fund 1923

37. *Letitia Wilson Jordan Bacon.* 1888. 47½ x 27″. In the Brooklyn Museum Collection,
Dick S. Ramsey Fund

38. *Samuel Murray.* 1889. 24 x 20″. Collection Mr. John R. Mitchell

39. *Miss van Buren*. 1889. 45 x 32". Phillips Collection, Washington

40. *Portrait of Man with Red Necktie* (Dr. Joseph Leidy, Jr.). 1890. 39½ x 36″. The Newark Museum

41. *Dr. Horatio C. Wood.* 1889. 5′4″ x 4′2″. The Detroit Institute of Arts

42. *The Bohemian (Franklin Schenk)*. 1890. 24 x 20″. Philadelphia Museum of Art

43. *Professor Henry A. Rowland*. 1891. 6′1½″ x 4′5¼″. Addison Gallery of American Art, Phillips Academy, Andover

44. *The Concert Singer*. 1892. 14⅜ x 10⅜″. Philadelphia Museum of Art

45. Sketch for *The Concert Singer*. 1892. 14⅜″ x 10⅜″. Philadelphia Museum of Art

46. *William McDowell.* 1891. Watercolor, 28 x 22″. Private collection

47. *Frank Hamilton Cushing.* 1894-5. 8′6″ x 5′. The Thomas Gilcrease Institute of American History and Art

48. *Mrs. Frank Hamilton Cushing*. Ca. 1894-5. 26 x 22″. Philadelphia Museum of Art

49. *Walt Whitman*. 1887. 30 x 24″. The Pennsylvania Academy of Fine Arts

50. *Charles Linford, the Artist.* Ca. 1895. 4' x 3'. International Business Machines Corporation

51. *Maud Cook*. 1895. 24 x 20″. Collection Mr. Stephen C. Clark

52. *Portrait of a Lady (Mrs. James Mapes Dodge)*. 1896. 24½ x 20¼". Philadelphia Museum of Art

53. *Maybelle.* 1898. 24 x 18". Frye Art Museum

54. *The Agnew Clinic.* 1898. 6'2½" x 10'10½". University of Pennsylvania

55. Study for Head of Referee in *Taking the Count*. 1898. 20 x 16″. Babcock Galleries

56. *Taking the Count.* 1898. 8 x 7'. Yale University Art Gallery, Whitney Collections of Sporting Art

57. *Salutat*. 1898. 50 x 40″. Addison Gallery of American Art, Phillips Academy, Andover

58. *Wrestlers.* 1889. 3'11" x 4'11". National Academy of Design

59. Oil sketch for *Wrestlers*. 1899. 3'4" x 4'2". Philadelphia Museum of Art

60. *Between Rounds*. 1899. 4′2″ x 3′4″. Philadelphia Museum of Art

61. *Benjamin Eakins*. 1899. 24 x 20″. Philadelphia Museum of Art

62. *Robert M. Lindsay.* 1900. 24 x 20″. The Detroit Institute of Arts

63. Oil sketch for portrait of *Robert M. Lindsay*. 1900. 11¾ x 10½". The Detroit Institute of Arts

64. *Cardinal Martinelli*. 1902. 6'7¼" x 5'. Catholic University of America

65. *Signora Gomez d'Arza*. 1902. 30 x 24″. The Metropolitan Museum of Art, George A. Hearn Fund, 1927

66. *Self Portrait*. 1902. 30 x 25". National Academy of Design

67. *The Young Man*. Ca. 1902. 45 x 26″. Philadelphia Museum of Art

68. *Mrs. M. S. Stokes.* 1903. 24 x 20". Canajoharie Library and Art Gallery

69. *Mrs. Anna M. Kershaw.* 1903. 24 x 20″. Collection Mr. Stephen C. Clark

70. *Music.* 1904. 3'3⅛" x 4' 1". Albright Art Gallery

71. *The Violinist.* 1904. 50 x 40". Collection Mr. Joseph Hirshhorn

72. *A. W. Lee*. 1905. 40 x 32″. Collection Mr. and Mrs. Lawrence A. Fleischman

73. *Monsignor Diomede Falconio.* 1905. 6′ x 46¼″. National Gallery of Art, Gift of Stephen C. Clark

74. *Old Fashioned Dress (Miss Parker)*. 1905. 5'⅜" x 3'4¼". Philadelphia Museum of Art

75. Prof. William Smith Forbes. 1905. 7 x 4′. Jefferson Medical College

76. *William Rush and His Model.* 1908. 3 x 4′. Honolulu Academy of Arts

77. *William Rush Carving His Allegorical Figure of the Skuylkill River, #2.* 1908. 3 x 4'.
In the Brooklyn Museum Collection, Dick S. Ramsey Fund

78. *Miss Elinor S. F. Pue*. 1908. 20 x 16″. The Virginia Museum of Fine Arts

79. *Ernest Lee Parker*. 1910. 24 x 20". Collection unknown

80. *Mrs. Gilbert Parker*. 1910. 24 x 20″. Museum of Fine Arts, Boston

Photograph George Eastman House

THOMAS EAKINS AND PHOTOGRAPHY

THE MOTION PICTURE and photography, like so many twentieth century phenomena, owe their current perfection to the painstaking and often anonymous research of nineteenth century pioneers who pushed back the frontiers of technology. Although the photographic process dates back to 1839 and Daguerre, photography was still in its infancy in the closing decades of the nineteenth century, a subject for experts and not the general public.

Eakins was interested in photography all his life. Since he based his art on the materialism of the nineteenth century, and since he liked tools, as more reliable than his free hand or free observation, the camera, in spite of its limitations which he knew very well, in his opinion was probably on a par with the mechanical draftsman's tools that he liked to use.

As a painter he concentrated on scenes from ordinary life. His

113

Photograph George Eastman House

scrupulous notions about the dignity of the exact and literal truth did not allow him to flatter people. The usefulness of the camera was limited for him by its accuracy and by his belief that observation goes only so far, and is no substitute for intelligence.

In fact, Eakins was himself an excellent photographer and between 1884 and 1885 undertook an epoch-making series of photographic studies of the human body in motion. Although Eakins would have been the last person to claim the invention of the motion picture camera, the fact remains that he worked out its basic principles at this early date.

Eakins' attraction to photography was based on more than just his artistic philosophy. He thought the naked human body the most beautiful thing in nature. This, coupled with a love of animals, particularly dogs and horses, and an amateur's preoccupation with science and technology was to lead to his photographic experiments.

In 1879 Fairman Rogers, a prominent Philadelphia art patron,

114

Photograph George Eastman House

commissioned Eakins to paint a picture of him driving in a coach. Eakins, an excellent rider and horse lover, made extensive studies for the painting. The coach was driven before him again and again, he painted several sketches of the horses, and he made individual wax models of the animals. The end product was a painting as accurate as a photograph.

Eakins had long been a keen observor of animal motion. He had made extensive studies of the muscles of horses, dogs, and cats, dissecting them and making casts of them. His scientific bent would not permit him to take any physiological idea on authority. When in doubt he tested all ideas relevant to the problems of accurate and realistic representation. One such unchallenged idea was that all four legs of a galloping horse are extended symmetrically.

The governor of California, Leland Stanford, employed the photographer Eadweard Muybridge to take pictures of galloping horses after making a $25,000 bet with a sporting friend about a horse's gait. Muybridge devised a battery of 24 cameras arranged

115

side by side along a track. By setting off the cameras in rapid succession as the horses galloped past he was able to take a series of photographs of the successive phases of their motion.

Eakins, no doubt intrigued by this new possibility of studying the human and animal figure in motion, took a close interest in these experiments and corresponded with Muybridge. When several wealthy Philadelphians guaranteed the necessary funds, Muybridge continued his experiments at the University of Pennsylvania in 1884, using human beings and birds as well as horses. Eakins was appointed a member of the supervising committee.

Muybridge, an expert photographer rather than a scientist, continued to use several cameras. Convinced of the inaccuracy of this method, Eakins began experimenting on a more scientific device on his own. He saw the advantage of using one camera and devised an apparatus with two disks, one moving eight times as fast as the other, revolving in front of the lens. This insured a series of nine or ten images on one plate. As a result it was possible to take a picture of a running figure and to produce successive, distinguishable images.

With this new device Eakins began an independent series of experiments in the fall of 1884, utilizing nude athletes and horses. In the spring of 1885 he gave illustrated lectures on the motions of the horse at the Pennsylvania Academy, using a zoëtrope, a precursor of the motion picture projector. Incredible as it may seem, this original and prophetic contribution went entirely unnoticed. But it is evident that Muybridge learned a great deal from his colleague's experimentation. For, despite the fact that Muybridge is an important name in the history of the motion picture and that Eakins is hardly ever mentioned in that connection, he eventually abandoned his own system of multiple cameras for the single camera method developed by Eakins.

Eakins never continued his experiments with moving figures after 1885. It is quite possible that he was primarily concerned with analyzing the motion of the human and animal body in connection with his artistic and anatomical preoccupations rather than synthe-

116

sizing the resulting images into moving pictures. Whatever his aim, however, he was in the vanguard of the photographic experimentation of his day, and he played an important, if unconscious, part in the long evolution of the motion picture.

CHRONOLOGY

1843	Benjamin Eakins, the son of a Scotch-Irish weaver, married Caroline Copperthwaite, the daughter of a Quaker cobbler.
1844	Thomas Eakins born July.
1846	The Eakins family moved to 1729 Mount Vernon Street, Philadelphia.
1861	Thomas Eakins graduated from Central High School with an A.B. degree. He refused to make a graduation address, saying that he had nothing original to say, and that he had learned everything from books, where others might find it.
1861–66	Studied drawing at the Pennsylvania Academy of Fine Arts and anatomy at Jefferson Medical School. He sailed for France in 1866.
1866	Entered Gérôme's class at the Ecole des Beaux Arts.
1869	Trip to Spain.
1870–72	Came home to Philadelphia to live all the rest of his life at 1729 Mount Vernon Street. Painted scenes of home life, particularly his sisters and their friends, until 1872, when his mother died.
1872	At his father's insistence that he was seeing too many girls and that he should settle down, he became engaged to Katherine Crowell.
1875	*The Gross Clinic.*
1876	Took over classes in anatomy at the Pennsylvania Academy of Fine Arts and taught without remuneration.
1879	Katherine Crowell died of meningitis. Made professor of anatomy at the Pennsylvania Academy.
1880	Joined the Society of American Artists.

1884	Married a pupil, Susan Hannah MacDowell, the daughter of an engraver. Series of experiments independent of the Muybridge work, under the auspices of the University of Pennsylvania.
1885	Gave a lecture illustrated on a zoetrope about the movements of a horse.
1886	Resigned from the Academy because of the scandal precipitated by his taking the loin cloth off a male model in the women's class.
	His pupils organized the Philadelphia Art Students' League, so they might still study under him. To help the school, he charged nothing for his services.
	Samuel Murray became his pupil at the Art Students' League, the beginning of a life-long friendship.
1887	Spent a summer on a ranch in Dakota.
1888–94	Taught at the National Academy of Design in New York.
1902	Unanimously elected to the National Academy, and made an Academician two months later.
1904	Received the Temple Gold Medal from the Pennsylvania Academy of Fine Arts.
1912	Spontaneously honored at a reception at Lancaster, Pa., where he had gone to attend an opening of an exhibition that included the *Agnew Clinic*.
1914	Dr. Barnes paid just under $5,000 for his study of the Agnew Clinic, which was three times what he had ever been paid for a painting.
1916	Died June 25, at 1729 Mount Vernon Street, Philadelphia.

SELECTED BIBLIOGRAPHY

Albright, Adam Emory: "Memories of Thomas Eakins, as told to Evelyn Marie Stuart," *Harper's Bazaar,* August 1947.

Baldinger, Wallace S.: "The Art of Eakins, Homer, and Ryder: a Social Revaluation," *Art Quarterly,* Summer 1946, Detroit Institute of Arts (contains reproductions of both versions of *The Lady with a Setter Dog*).

Barker, Virgil: "Imagination in Thomas Eakins," *Parnassus,* November 1937.

Barnes, Albert C.: *The Art in Painting,* Barnes Foundation Press, Merion, Pa.

Beaux, Cecilia: *Background with Figures, the Autobiography of Cecilia Beaux,* Boston and New York, 1930.

Bregler, Charles: "Thomas Eakins as a Teacher," *The Arts,* March and October 1931.

Brownell, William C.: "The Art Schools of Philadelphia," *Scribner's Monthly Illustrated Magazine,* September 1879.

——— "The Younger Painters of America," *Scribner's Monthly Illustrated Magazine,* May 1880.

Burroughs, Allan: "Thomas Eakins the Man," *The Arts,* December 1923.

Caffin, Charles H.: "Some American Portrait Painters," *The Critic,* January 1904.

Cortissoz, Royal: *American Artists,* New York, 1923.

Current Opinion, Dec. 1917, "Thomas Eakins, Another Neglected Master of American Art."

Eakins, Thomas: *Animal Locomotion, The Muybridge Work at the University of Pennsylvania; the Method and the Result,* Philadelphia, 1888 (containing a description by Eakins of his apparatus).

——— *Catalogue of a Loan Exhibition of the Works of Thomas Eakins,* the Metropolitan Museum of Art, New York, 1917. With an introduction by Bryson Burroughs.

——— *Catalogue of a Memorial Exhibition of the Works of the Late Thomas Eakins,* Pennsylvania Academy of the Fine Arts, Philadelphia, 1917. With an introduction by Gilbert Sunderland Parker.

121

—— "On the Differential Action of Certain Muscles Passing More than One Joint," *Proceedings of the Academy of Natural Sciences of Philadelphia,* 1894.

—— *Thomas Eakins Centennial, a Catalogue of a Loan Exhibition of the Works of Thomas Eakins,* M. Knoedler and Co., New York, 1944.

Eggers, George W.: "Thomas Eakins 1844–1916," *Bulletin of the Worcester Art Museum,* January 1930.

Flexner, James Thomas: *Thomas Eakins,* Metropolitan Museum of Art Miniatures, New York, 1956. 24 colored illus.

Goodrich, Lloyd: *Thomas Eakins, His Life and Work,* Whitney Museum, New York, 1933. The most complete biography. 224 pages, 72 plates, a catalogue of his works, and a bibliography.

—— "Thomas Eakins Today," *Magazine of Art,* May 1944.

Gutman, Walter: "Thomas Eakins and his Art," *New York Sun,* November 16, 1929.

Hartman, Sadakichi: *A History of American Art,* Boston, 1902.

Henri, Robert: *The Art Spirit,* Philadelphia and New York, 1923.

LaFollette, Suzanne: *Art in America,* New York, 1929.

Mather, Frank Jewett, Jr.: *Estimates in Art,* New York, 1931.

McBride, Henry: "Exhibitions at New York Galleries," *Fine Arts Journal,* December 1917.

—— "Modern Art," *The Dial,* January 1926.

McHenry, Margaret: *Thomas Eakins, Who Painted,* privately issued, Oreland, Pa., 1946. Contains much material that is not in Goodrich. 162 mimeographed pages, Whitman bibliography, and bibliography of Eakins letters.

Meyer, Anne Nathan: "Two Portraits of Walt Whitman," *Putnam's Monthly* and *The Reader,* September 1908.

Mumford, Lewis: *The Brown Decades,* Dover Publications, Inc., New York 10, N.Y. ($1.65).

Rogers, Fairman: "The Schools of the Pennsylvania Academy of the Fine Arts," *The Pennsylvania Monthly,* June 1881.

Pach, Walter: *Ananias, or the False Artist,* New York, 1928.

—— "A Grand Provincial," in the *Freeman Book,* New York, 1924.

Pennell, Joseph: *Adventures of an Illustrator,* Boston, 1925.

Traubel, Horace, *With Walt Whitman in Camden,* Boston, 1906–53. 4 vols.

Van Rensselaer, M. G.: *Book of American Figure Painters,* Philadelphia, 1886 (contains a reproduction of the first version, that Eakins painted over, of *The Lady with a Setter Dog*).

122

PHOTOGRAPHIC CREDITS

The photographs in this book are reproduced through the courtesy of those listed below:

Addison Gallery of American Art, Phillips Academy, Andover   43
Babcock Galleries   4, 16, 33, 35, 46, 51, 55, 71
Brenwasser Photographer   9, 68
Brooklyn Museum   5, 12, 37
Cleveland Museum of Art   11
Detroit Institute of Art   40, 62, 63
Frick Art Reference Library   2, 6, 15, 30, 58, 59, 66, 72, 79
Frye Art Museum   53
Thomas Gilcrease Institute of American History & Art   47
Lloyd Goodrich   75
Kleemann Galleries   69, 76
Metropolitan Museum of Art   13, 14, 22, 23, 28, 36, 56, 65
Charles P. Mills & Son   20
Museum of Art, Rhode Island School of Design   19
Museum of Fine Arts, Boston   80
National Gallery of Art   27, 73
Philadelphia Museum of Art   1, 3, 7, 10, 29, 31, 42, 44, 45, 48, 52, 60, 61, 67, 74
Phillips Collection, Washington   39
Sandak, Inc.   17, 21, 25, 57
Time, Inc.   8, 32, 77
Virginia Museum of Fine Arts   78

INDEX

The roman numerals refer to text references, the *italic* numerals to the black and white plates, and the **bold face** numerals to the color plates. The titles of the reproductions are listed in *italics*.

125

126

WESTMAR COLLEGE LIBRARY